CUTTING-EDGE TECHNOLOGY

MAGLEV TRAINS

Shanghai Transrapid

Louise and Richard Spilsbury

Gareth Stevens
PUBLISHING

Please visit our website, **www.garethstevens.com**.
For a free color catalog of all our high-quality books,
call toll free 1-800-542-2595 or fax 1-877-542-2596.

Cataloging-in-Publication Data
Names: Spilsbury, Louise.
Title: Maglev trains / Louise and Richard Spilsbury.
Description: New York : Gareth Stevens Publishing, 2017. | Series: Cutting-edge technology | Includes index.
Identifiers: ISBN 9781482451658 (pbk.) | ISBN 9781482451597 (library bound) | ISBN 9781482451474 (6 pack)
Subjects: LCSH: High speed trains–Juvenile literature.
Classification: LCC TF1450.S65 2017 | DDC 385'.2–dc23

First Edition

Published in 2017 by
Gareth Stevens Publishing
111 East 14th Street, Suite 349
New York, NY 10003

© 2017 Gareth Stevens Publishing

Produced for Gareth Stevens by Calcium
Editors: Sarah Eason and Harriet McGregor
Designer: Jessica Moon
Picture researcher: Harriet McGregor

Picture credits: Cover: WikimediShutterstock: Eky Studio (banner), Shutterstock: R-studio (back cover bkgrd); Insides: Shutterstock: ChameleonsEye 1, 5, 19, Forance 11, Sean Pavone 33, Stanislav Sergeev 37, Joseph Sohm 31, SSSCCC 17, Bernhard Staehli 45, YMZK-Photo 14; Thyssenkrupp: 41; Wikimedia Commons: Fortheworld 21, Jorg Hackemann 35, Hisagi 27, Maryland GovPics 25, Morio 39, NASA 43, Lars Plougmann 13, Colin Rose 9, Sakaori/National Land Image Information (Color Aerial Photographs), Ministry of Land, Infrastructure, Transport and Tourism, Japan 28, Ssguy 23, U.S. National Archives and Records Administration 7.

Printed in the United States of America

CPSIA compliance information: Batch #CS16GS: For further information contact Gareth Stevens, New York, New York at 1-800-542-2595.

CONTENTS

CHAPTER 1

MAGLEV TRAINS

A train pulls into the station. Its arrival is quiet and smooth. There is no roar of an engine or squeal of metal wheels on the track. In fact, the train glides in, floating above the rails. This is not science fiction! There are trains like this in operation today. Floating trains use maglev technology.

WHAT IS MAGLEV?

"Maglev" is a word made up from two others: "magnetic" and "levitation." The train is lifted, or levitated, into the air using magnetism. Magnetism is a force that can pull or push on an object. It can be used to push up a train, but more commonly is used for things like keeping a refrigerator door closed.

ADVANTAGES OF MAGLEV

Any object being pushed or pulled in one direction encounters other forces in the other direction that slow it down. A train wheel rolling forward on rails has a contact force called **friction** that works backward to slow the wheel. Regular trains have a lot of wheels so they need a lot of engine power to make them move forward. Maglev trains have no wheels so they are not in contact with the tracks, or guideways as they are known. There is no friction to slow them. With no contact, the train will not skid if the tracks are icy.

The magnetism that lifts maglev trains is also used to make the trains move along tracks. This means they have no heavy engine on board, which makes maglev trains lighter than regular trains, even though they do carry powerful magnets. Being lighter means maglevs need less power to move fast.

BETTER UP HILLS

Vehicles struggle to move up inclines, or slopes, because another force acts on them. This is the downward force of gravity, which pulls the vehicles' mass backward down the tracks. Wheeled trains stop or even slip backward on slopes. Maglev trains can move up slopes because they have no track friction and a smaller mass for gravity to act on.

Shanghai Transrapid

A maglev train quietly arrives at a station in Shanghai, China. The potential of travel using the forces of magnetism is already a reality in some parts of the world.

FLOATING TRAINS

Maglev trains are a modern transportation technology, but they have a history that stretches back about 100 years. The floating trains of today are possible because of the pioneering work of inventors in the past.

MAGLEV HISTORY

One hundred years ago, electrical machines were much rarer than today. People were looking for new ways to use electricity. In 1905, German inventor Alfred Zehden (1876–1933) invented an electric motor to pull cable cars along a rail or trains along a track using magnets. Emile Bachelet (1863–1946) was a Frenchman who moved to the United States in the 1880s to work as an electrician. Bachelet experimented with magnets powered by electricity to treat patients with arthritis. He figured out how to use multiple magnetic forces to lift and push objects along. In 1912, he published plans for a machine that would use magnets to transfer mail at high speed.

MONORAILS AND "HOVERCRAFT"

By 1934, another German inventor named Hermann Kemper (1892–1977) had developed detailed plans for a monorail vehicle with no wheels that could transport people. Then, in the late 1950s, Eric Laithwaite (1921–1997) of Manchester University, England, built a full-scale working model of a linear motor using powerful magnets. This used the same principles as Zehden's motor (of nearly half a century earlier) to move a train forward without any contact. Laithwaite's invention was known as the "Tracked Hovercraft," and its technology is the basis of that used by most maglev trains today.

In a quiet desert area in Pueblo, Colorado, in 1973, a scientist tests out a prototype maglev train on a test track.

EUREKA!

In 1960, student James R. Powell sat in his automobile trapped in gridlock traffic on a bridge in New York State and dreamed of a better, less polluting way to travel. This spurred Powell and a coworker, Gordon Danby, to invent a maglev system of trains and tracks, or guideways, building on the earlier ideas of Emile Bachelet. In the late 1960s and 1970s, working models were developed, but their maglev dream has still not become reality in the United States.

On August 16, 1984, passengers stepped onto a shuttle service between Birmingham International Airport, England, and its nearest railway station. This journey of 2,000 feet (600 m) at a speed of 25 miles (40 km) per hour was the first commercial maglev transportation service.

Many countries had shown great interest in the maglev technology demonstrated by Laithwaite and by Powell and Danby. But investment in the technology had been delayed, partly as a result of the great costs involved.

BIRMINGHAM INTERNATIONAL AIRPORT

The Birmingham International Airport maglev was funded by the British government and developed for five years before use. However, it was closed down in 1995. One problem was that engineers decided the railcars were not strong enough, so they reinforced them with glass fiber, a very tough material made from strands of glass glued together. This made the railcars too heavy for the original magnets to lift so they needed expensive new magnets! The airport shuttle was too expensive to maintain and repair, so it was replaced with a bus.

M-BAHN

In 1983, construction began on the **M-Bahn** in Berlin, Germany. At that time, the Berlin Wall separated West Berlin from East Berlin. The M-Bahn was to run only in areas of West Berlin, where a railroad had been cut when the Wall was built in 1961. Then, in 1989, the two halves of Berlin were reunited. The Wall was knocked down. Politicians decided that the original train line should be reconnected and that the M-Bahn was in the way. It was dismantled in 1992.

At Expo '86 in Vancouver, Canada, fairgoers had a taste of transportation of the future when they took magnetic rides on the first working maglev in North America.

SHOW RIDES

Some of the first maglevs were fairground rides. One maglev test track of 0.25 mile (400 m) was built in Vancouver, Canada, for the 1986 World's Fair, or Expo '86. The theme of Expo '86 was transportation, and other attractions included the SkyTrain monorail. The maglev was dismantled after the show, but today a SkyTrain network connects a lot of Vancouver.

CHAPTER 2

HOW MAGLEVS WORK

A maglev train can weigh around 50 tons (45 mt) and carry passengers and baggage weighing many more tons. How can magnets lift such heavy weights?

The magnetic forces in a magnet are strongest at its ends, which are called poles. One is the north pole and one is the south pole. If two magnets are brought together, a north pole pulls toward a south pole. However, two north or two south poles **repel** one another. The stronger the magnet, the greater the attraction or repulsion. These effects are found in an area around the magnet called a **magnetic field.**

POWER MAGNETS

Some magnets permanently have magnetic fields because they have areas of magnetic forces called domains inside them that line up and face the same direction. Other magnets can be turned off or on by a switch. When electricity flows through a wire, domains form, line up,

CUTTING EDGE

Some of today's **superconductors** can work well at temperatures of around −230 degrees Fahrenheit (−145°C). They are kept cool using tanks of liquid nitrogen, which are generally available and not expensive to buy.

Magnetic levitation is shown here using a superconducting magnet containing liquid nitrogen. The clouds are caused by the low temperatures of the nitrogen freezing water molecules in the air.

and create a small magnetic field around the wire. Winding many wires together makes a stronger field. Magnets created by the flow of electricity are called **electromagnets**. In maglev trains, powerful electromagnets are used to create magnetic fields that hold the train above its guideway.

Superconductors allow electricity to flow through them far better than pure metals. However, they only superconduct if they are cooled down. Most maglev train electromagnets are made from coils of superconducting wire. The electromagnets must be kept very cold to make the magnets strong enough.

Not all maglev trains are the same. There are three ways in which maglev trains float along their guideways. The most common maglev technology is called **electromagnetic suspension (EMS)**. In EMS maglev trains, the railcars have arms beneath them that wrap around the guideway. The arms are C-shaped in cross-section and the lower part of the "C" contains electromagnets. The guideway is made of steel and often T-shaped in cross-section. Power from batteries on board the train turn on the electromagnets. This attracts the electromagnets to the guideway. The magnetic force overcomes gravity, causing the magnetic train arms to lift up. The cars rise by up to 0.5 inch (1 cm).

NONSTICK

The train must not stick to its guideway. There are more magnets built into the inner edge of the arms along both sides of the railcars. These magnets are attracted inward from both sides toward the guideway. This makes the railcar arms stay at a fixed distance from the guideway. Sensors monitor the gaps between train and guideway. Information from the sensors is used by electronic systems to adjust the magnet strength so the train never touches its guideway.

MOVING FORWARD

All along the guideway on each side are sequences of electromagnets that can be made to create north and south poles. Magnets with fixed poles at the front and back of the railcars are alternately attracted or repelled by the guideway magnets. This arrangement pushes the train from behind and pulls it from the front, so it moves forward.

You can see the arms at the side of the maglev cars wrapping around the guideway on this EMS maglev train in Shanghai, China.

CUTTING EDGE

EMS maglev trains never run out of battery power and slump onto their guideway. The carriage arms have **generators** built into the support magnets. These devices recharge the batteries as the train moves past them. Even if this fails, the EMS carriages carry emergency batteries to keep the trains from stopping or losing control.

PUSHED AWAY

EMS technology is all about attraction, but the other main maglev system relies on repulsion. The **electrodynamic suspension (EDS)** system uses magnetic fields on both the train and on the guideway to raise the train.

An EDS train often runs inside a walled guideway, which has coils of wire that run along its length. Beneath the train's cars are superconductor electromagnets. These magnets are so powerful that they create magnetic fields in the guideway coils as the train approaches.

Magnets in the walled guideway for this train both push the railcars away and forward at high speeds toward their destination.

HAZARDS

The magnetic fields on an EMS train are about the same as those around an operating hair dryer. However, magnetic fields from superconductor electromagnets on an EDS train are many times stronger. These fields could destroy laptop hard drives and information on credit cards, and even affect pacemakers implanted in people to treat heart problems. For this reason, EDS trains have layers of magnetic shielding materials in the floor to protect passengers.

The fields grow stronger the faster the train moves. This is called **electromagnetic induction**. The magnetic fields in the guideway and in the train repel each other. The train rises as long as the upward magnetic force is greater than gravity.

An EDS maglev train is pulled forward by electromagnets in the guideway. Moving railcars induce currents in the coils, creating magnetic fields around the coils. These changing fields attract and repel the cars to keep the train moving.

SPEED FOR LIFT
Unless the maglev train is moving fast, the magnetic fields will be too small to lift it. So, at the start and end of each journey, the EMS train moves along on wheels. The wheels lift up above the track when the train is moving fast enough to induce magnetic fields and raise its cars.

The third maglev train technology does not use electromagnets at all! The **Inductrack** system is not yet in use anywhere in the world, but it has been tested. It uses permanent magnets with virtually no need for power. Inductrack relies on magnetic repulsion. The Inductrack permanent magnets are arranged in a particular way called a **Halbach array**. A single magnet has an equal strength magnetic field on either side. A Halbach array is several single magnets arranged in different ways to produce a strong magnetic field on one side and a weak field on the other. These magnets can direct magnetic force in one direction only.

CREATING LIFT

In the Inductrack technology, the Halbach magnets are on the underside of the train and its guideway contains coils of metal wire. The train begins to move using a small electric motor, which turns the train's wheels. The array induces magnetic fields in the guideway, which repel those from the array. The repulsion lifts the train up. Inductrack trains levitate at much slower speeds than EDS trains, making them suitable for urban use.

CUTTING EDGE

Halbach arrays were originally developed to construct machines called particle accelerators, which scientists use to study the secrets of the universe. In the future, they might have a use in medicine. Scientists want to use these magnets to direct drugs into body parts that need them. The Halbach arrays could direct tiny pieces of magnetized drugs into particular organs.

The Hadron Collider is a huge particle accelerator. Its powerful magnetic arrays can shoot particles through its insides as fast as going around the world 7.5 times in 1 second!

CHAPTER 3

COMMERCIAL MAGLEVS

Maglev technology is not new. Commercial trains have existed since the 1980s. However, there are few working maglevs today and the oldest of these runs in Shanghai, China. This maglev started its service between Pudong International Airport and downtown Shanghai in 2004.

TRANSRAPID

The Shanghai maglev is based on German maglev technology. The German government, with industrial partners, had invested in developing a high-speed train using EMS technology. To do this, they created a company called Transrapid. Transrapid tested the train through the 1990s, achieving a world speed record of 279 miles (450 km) per hour in 1993.

AIRPORT CONNECTION

Late in 1999, the Shanghai government approached German companies to help them use Transrapid for a high-speed line connecting their international airport and Longyang Road metro station. This was seen as a priority for air passengers arriving in the city, who needed to connect with other parts of the country by existing railroad networks. Construction began in 2001 and the 19-mile (30 km) route was in operation just three years later!

Commuters take their regular smooth and silent trip from the airport to downtown Shanghai on the maglev train.

COOPERATION

The Shanghai maglev was built by German and Chinese engineers working together on the project. The railcars were built in ThyssenKrupp factories in Kassel, Germany. Other German companies made the electromagnets, and others the guideway. All of these were shipped to China. Chinese engineers built the guideway, with help from German experts.

The Shanghai Transrapid maglev uses electromagnets to attract the railcars up to the guideway to hover like other EMS systems. The Transrapid uses less power to hover than it uses in its air conditioning equipment for passengers inside. It can hover for up to one hour on battery power without any need for recharging.

PROPULSION

The Transrapid is pulled along by a traveling magnetic field created along the length of the guideway. To change speed, the strength of the current running through the coils is altered. To brake, the Transrapid reverses the direction of the traveling magnetic field. Electricity is actually generated by this process and is used to recharge the batteries.

SAFETY

Transrapid maglevs are almost impossible to derail. This is because the arms of the railcars wrap around the guideway. There is also almost no chance of a collision between trains. The magnetic field in the guideway means that if two trains are on it, they must travel in the same direction.

OPERATION CONTROL

The operation control system monitors the trains' locations using sensors on the trains that detect electronic flags positioned along the guideway. It monitors the speed, guideway clearance of the train, and other information. The information is sent between the train and a control center on the ground using radio transmission. This allows constant communication between the driver and the control center.

LongYang Road station was built in the air to meet the guideways of the maglev, which were raised up to avoid the existing train lines on the ground.

CUTTING EDGE

There are two reinforced concrete guideways in Shanghai for the Transrapid. Trains can move between guideways to allow them to pass one another. This happens using switches. In these switches, electromagnets pull the ends of steel beam sections of guideway, causing them to bend. The guideways are then securely locked at their ends before a train can change route.

The Shanghai Transrapid maglev trains speed passengers from airport to station in less than eight minutes. They hit top speeds of almost 270 miles (430 km) per hour during the journey, although on test runs this maglev can travel at 310 miles (500 km) per hour.

There are three Shanghai Transrapid maglev trains, each made up of six cars. They are 500 feet (153 m) long and almost 12 feet (4 m) wide. The front and back cars include a section in which the driver works. These cars have slightly angled noses with a windshield. They have lights to illuminate the guideway during night services. With no engine, the rest of the space in the end railcars is for seating. Other cars have blunt ends and are for passengers only. Each train can carry 574 passengers.

EXTENDED SERVICE

Maglev services run every 10 or 15 minutes from 6:45 a.m. until 9:30 p.m. The train had too few passengers at first because its hours of operation were too short to include connection with popular early and late flights at the airport.

SHANGHAI COSTS

The Shanghai maglev cost $1.2 billion to build in three years. Passengers can buy a one-way ticket for $8. By 2013, the maglev had been used for about 40 million passenger journeys. This means that, so far, the Shanghai maglev has earned only part of what it cost to build.

The spread of maglev routes from Shanghai Pudong to other parts of the country is currently on hold, but maybe in the future air passengers will be able to connect with more of China by maglev.

Shanghai's government planned to extend the maglev line to other airports near the city and neighboring Hangzhou. This would have increased connections in a much wider region. In 2006, the Chinese government approved the plans, but soon afterward a decision was made to not start construction. Instead, the Ministry of Transport in Beijing wanted to use the investment money for conventional rail projects linking a wider part of the country than just in Shanghai. As it later turned out, the fastest train in the world was not to be Chinese, but instead Japanese.

CHAPTER 4

THE FASTEST TRAIN IN THE WORLD

In summer 2015, the passengers on a sleek Japanese train applauded when it reached a new world record top speed. The fastest train in the world was the L0 **shinkansen** maglev train owned by the Central Japan Railway Company. Its record-breaking speed was 374 miles (603 km) per hour.

HISTORY

Japan has a long history of fast trains. In the nineteenth century, Japan was already planning a high-speed train between Tokyo and Yokohama. However, a lack of money and two world wars interrupted plans. In the 1960s, the Japanese government started a program of high-speed rail development.

GAME CHANGER

The first shinkansen trains were the 0 series that began service in 1964. They could travel at 137 miles (220 km) per hour, which cut the rail journey from Tokyo to Osaka from 6 hours and 40 minutes to 3 hours and 10 minutes. More high-speed railroads were built, and there have been many generations of shinkansens. Most were conventional trains with diesel engines, but maglev technology was developed in Japan, too. Japanese engineers developed the EDS maglev system, and in 2003, they took the world high-speed rail record from the Shanghai maglev with a speed of 361 miles (581 km) per hour.

The test track in Japan showcases the L0 shinkansen maglev train. Government representatives travel from other countries to experience a test ride on board this high-speed maglev.

FAST NAME

"Shinkansen" means "new trunk line" because many high-speed trains of the past could only run on new networks of tracks. In the 1930s, engineers discussing high-speed trains in Japan called them bullet trains for their speed. The design of the 0 series shinkansen in the 1960s had distinctive curved noses that resembled a bullet. The name "bullet train" stuck!

DESIGNED FOR SPEED

The most obvious design feature of the Japanese L0 shinkansen maglev is its long nose. The nose takes up about half of the length of the front car. This smooth, tapering design feature helps make the L0 **aerodynamic**.

An aerodynamic shape helps a vehicle move fast through the air with less **drag**. This is especially important when fast trains hit air trapped inside tunnels. The plug of air in the tunnel is pushed ahead of the train and slows its progress. However, the long nose of the L0 and the train's square cross-section prevent it from losing speed and reduce its energy use at high speeds. The L0 is made of light materials, which means less power is needed for the magnets to lift the train. Scientists have calculated that the L0 uses 30 percent less energy than a Transrapid maglev when traveling at similar speeds.

COMFORT AND STABILITY

A fast passenger train needs to offer a comfortable ride to the people inside. Attraction between magnets at the edges of the guideway and under the L0 keeps the train stable as it glides along. This effect grows stronger as the train moves faster, because the magnetic force is induced in the guideway by the approaching train.

The repulsion that keeps the EDS maglev in the air also increases the faster it goes. In fact, the force is too weak to lift up the train at low speeds. That is why the L0 leaves and arrives back at stations on rubber wheels. The wheels automatically fold up beneath the train when it speeds above 93 miles (150 km) per hour and fold down again when it slows. The wheels also deploy if power to the train is cut during an emergency, so it can come to a halt safely.

CUTTING EDGE

In Switzerland, engineers and designers planning a national maglev high-speed rail network have figured out a way to reduce drag even further. They plan to pump out the air from the tunnels containing the maglev guideways as they wind through the country's mountains. With little air in tunnels, speeds could hit 621 miles (1,000 km) per hour!

The remarkable L0 shinkansen has been tried and tested and is now ready to be deployed through Japan on a new network of guideways that should start operation by 2027.

JAPANESE NETWORK

The shinkansen test track is in a built-up area of Japan. An extra benefit of the aerodynamic shape is a quieter ride, because more drag causes more noise.

The L0 is an impressive piece of technology, but one that many passengers cannot pay to ride on. Currently, it speeds along a test track near Mount Fuji. In the near future, it could be part of Central Japan Railway Company's planned high-speed network across the country.

In 2014, engineers began work constructing the maglev guideway for a line connecting Tokyo and Nagoya that will use L0 shinkansen trains. This section of the line should be completed by 2027. The two cities are 178 miles (286 km) apart. By then, commuters should be able to complete the journey in just 40 minutes.

The Tokyo–Nagoya route is a major challenge to engineers because 85 percent of its distance will be through new tunnels. The surface land between the cities has little space for a direct line. The Tokyo and Nagoya stations will need to be 131 feet (40 m) underground because the cities are so built up. Building underground costs more than building on the surface. It requires special digging equipment and extremely strong tunnels to support the weight of land above.

WORTH THE PRICE

The Japanese maglev shinkansen line should be extended farther west to Osaka by 2045. By then, the Central Japan Railway Company expects to have spent an incredible $74.7 billion on the project. They believe that it is worth the cost. The shinkansen trains are fast, but not as fast as airplanes. However, shinkansen passengers can complete a journey of a given length more quickly than air passengers because they do not have to spend time checking in at airports. Rail travel is also very safe and is not canceled during bad weather.

CUTTING EDGE

Japan is in a part of the world in which there are frequent large earthquakes. This means Japanese companies need construction that help them survive the quakes. The shinkansen maglev EDS technology has a high ground clearance, so the train should not scrape on the ground during an earthquake. As long as there is power for the electromagnets, the train should float.

CHAPTER 5

URBAN MAGLEVS

Cities are growing worldwide. Today, more than half the world's population lives in urban areas and there are more than 400 cities of over 1 million people. Urban transportation has a big impact on urban living. It is a major challenge keeping people moving in and around cities without creating problems such as air pollution. Maglev trains are one solution to these problems.

INCREASED TRAFFIC

Urban transportation has changed throughout history. In the nineteenth century, horse-drawn carriages, trams, and underground trains were popular. When cars became cheap enough for people to buy, city planners built more highways in and around cities. Today, road traffic dominates and causes problems in many cities. It results in gridlock morning and night, and poisonous gases and dirt from engines cause major health problems, such as asthma. Many cities are investing in public transportation systems, like subways and cable cars, to get people off the roads.

MAGLEV FOR CITIES

Maglevs have an especially low environmental impact. They have no engines causing air pollution. They use just a small amount of electricity during operation. Maglev trains can be as noisy as regular trains at high speeds because of the drag. However, maglevs can hardly be heard when traveling at less than 125 miles (201 km) per hour because they have no engines. This is a great benefit for lines through urban residential areas.

This is gridlock on Pasadena Freeway into downtown Los Angeles; in the future, could this be a thing of the past with better urban transportation such as maglev trains?

THRU TRAFFIC MERGE RIGHT

EXIT 24B
Civic Center
Hill Street
ONLY

110
Downtown

EXIT 24C
Dodger
Stadium
EXIT 1/4 MI

NAVAL AND
MARINE CORPS
RESERVE CENTER
NEXT EXIT

COMMUTERS

Commuters in Nagoya, Japan, have been using maglev trains for their day-to-day journeys back and forth to work since 2005. The **Linimo** maglev runs between 9 stations along a 5.5-mile (9 km) line. Its top speed is only 60 miles (100 km) per hour. It uses EMS technology to transport 4,000 passengers in each direction every hour. It is so popular that in 2005 there were two occasions when the number of passengers was so great the train could not float!

South Korea is a highly advanced country in East Asia. In general, South Koreans are well paid, have world-class education and healthcare, and the world's fastest Internet. They also live in a country in which more is spent on inventing new things per person than anywhere else. South Korea has invented its own maglev urban transportation system.

FIRST SERVICES

South Korea's work on maglev technology began in the 1990s, funded by the government. Teams of inventors and engineers at Hyundai-Rotem researched and developed a new type of EMS maglev, a little like the Linimo maglev of Japan. The first operating urban maglev in Korea was tested in 1993. It has run on a 0.62-mile (1 km) guideway between the National Science Museum and Expo Park in the city of Daejeon since 2008. The first commercial maglev train service began in 2015 and connected Incheon International Airport in Seoul with the nearby islands of Yongyoo-Muui.

FUTURE TRAFFIC?

The line out to the islands of Yongyoo-Muui was put there for the future. There were plans to convert the Yongyoo-Muui islands into a gigantic new tourist city, named EightCity. The government and private investors planned to spend $264 billion on the project. The hope was to attract millions of tourists each year to Korea. However, interest in the project was not great enough and plans are on hold. Maglev is still slowly expanding in Korea, though. The airport link connects part of the area around Incheon Airport, and the maglev line around Daejeon will be expanded to serve a wider area.

Seoul, the capital of South Korea, is a very modern city that is expanding fast. It hopes to improve urban transportation and entice more visitors by expanding its maglev network.

EIGHTCITY

EightCity was to be a giant city with eight parts dedicated to activities. It was to be made up of hotels, conference centers, malls, theme parks, a medical healing town, and even a Formula One racetrack. There would be a tubular building more than 8 miles (14 km) long. The modern maglev trains would have been the ideal form of transportation for this modern tourism center.

It is currently impossible to find any working maglev trains outside East Asian cities. This technology is only in use in China, Japan, and South Korea. But urban maglevs are likely to spread outside this region in the next few decades.

RUSSIA

In 2014, the Russian government signed an agreement to bring maglev to Russia. The new train line will use Korean technology to connect with St. Petersburg Metro Line 4 at a station called Narodnaya and also a regional bus terminal. One of the investment companies, Gordon Atlantic, plans to build a retail village on the new line in which passengers can shop. This will enable the investors to earn back some of their investment money from stores in the village.

INDONESIA AND THE UNITED STATES

The government of Jakarta in Indonesia is also considering a maglev line that would link the airport with downtown Jakarta.

In the United States, there is a proposed new maglev line between Washington, D.C. and

CUTTING EDGE

Maglevs are almost impossible to derail because they have magnets all along their length, holding them over the guideway as they travel. Part of the interest in maglev in the United States is the result of rail safety concerns. Early in 2015, an Amtrak train derailed traveling around a bend in Pittsburgh. The incident killed eight people and caused people to question the safety of fast regular trains.

New York City that could complete the journey in two hours. The Japanese government wants to export the technology behind the fastest train in the world and will invest money in this U.S. project. However, whether the planned line goes ahead or not will depend on U.S. politicians and the popularity of the line with the people who elect them. Car and air travel are also very popular in the United States, so there may not be enough public support for maglev trains.

EXPENSIVE TECHNOLOGY?

Maglev is expensive to develop from initial designs to working trains and guideways. One reason for this is that maglev technology and its systems are relatively new, so every part needs to be specially made.

Maglev guideways are complicated to put together because coils of wire and electromagnets must be linked inside steel or concrete structures. In the United States, the cost of part of the planned Washington–New York City maglev guideway between Baltimore and Washington is estimated at $8 billion. This route covers 39.8 miles (64.1 km). The cost is about $20 million per mile. Surprisingly, that is not greatly different to regular rail. In the United Kingdom, estimated costs of building a new high-speed regular rail service were more expensive than the maglev track.

VARYING COSTS

There are many reasons why different rail projects cost different amounts. Land costs and building costs vary depending on where land is and how mountainous or built-up it is. The cost of using different technologies varies too. For example, there are no steel wheels that rub and wear away on maglev tracks and they do not carry the weight of the train, so maintenance costs should be lower than for regular tracks.

TRAINS DELAYED

There are many maglev train projects that have either been canceled or delayed. In the United Kingdom, the government rejected maglev technology for a high-speed rail project partly because maglev trains could not shift from a guideway onto existing high-speed rail tracks to link with other parts of Europe.

Machinery works on a conventional rail. Surprisingly, the cost per mile of maglev guideway is no more expensive than the cost of building high-speed rail tracks.

CUTTING EDGE

Maglev trains can only reach their top speeds on long, straight sections of guideway. The world speed records in Japan took place on a straight test track. In reality, guideways may have to curve around buildings, or stations may be too close together for maglev trains to travel any faster than regular trains before they have to brake.

CHAPTER 6

NEW USES FOR MAGLEV

In laboratories around the world, scientists specializing in magnetic forces are researching new ideas for maglev technology. These include making faster and cheaper maglev train systems and looking at ways to apply maglev principles in other industries.

Maglev designers need test tracks. One of the earliest test tracks is in Emsland, Germany. This 13-mile (21 km) long test guideway has a test center next to it. There, scientists tested a vehicle called TR06. They altered the arrangement and power of the magnets, the shape of the railcar, and other parts. Through this testing process, they developed the Transrapid maglev system that is still in operation in Shanghai today. A similar test track at Yamanashi, Japan, was used to develop the high-speed shinkansen maglev.

FREIGHT SHIFTER

In San Diego, the only working maglev train in the United States is being used to carry shipping containers back and forth on a test Inductrack. This train is a black platform that glides smoothly along the 400-foot (130 m) long raised guideway. General Atomics is the company that invented Inductrack, and they have set up the test track to demonstrate the technology. They think that their technology could be used to move containers from ports to urban centers.

The L0 is the latest in a long line of maglev shinkansen designs tested out at the Yamanashi test track in Japan.

CUTTING EDGE

In a Barcelona skate park in summer 2015, a board without wheels hung in the air for a suspiciously long time. It was a maglev hoverboard. The track looked like a regular skate park but was actually a 655-foot (200 m) strip of magnetic track. Inside the board were superconductor magnets bathed in liquid nitrogen. The board rider floated about 2 inches (5 cm) above the track because the board repelled the track.

Maglev technology might also be used to carry objects vertically instead of just horizontally. The power of magnets could lift heavy objects without actually touching them. The days of cables and ropes to elevate things may be coming to an end.

ThyssenKrupp is one of the engineering companies behind the Transrapid maglev trains, but they also make elevators. Their latest invention is called MULTI, which is a maglev elevator! These elevators do not move at high speeds, but they can reduce waiting time for elevators. This is because the system could include many elevators able to move both horizontally and vertically and to pass each other in the same elevator shaft. This would be a huge advantage for tall buildings that rely on elevators for transporting people inside. Regular elevators with their motors, cables, and multiple shafts can take up a large amount of a building's internal space. The MULTI elevator shafts would take up just half of this space.

THEME PARK MAGLEV

Magnetic forces are being used in some theme parks. Roller coasters must get up high to start their runs. Usually they rely on chains that move between the tracks under the power of electric motors. The cars hook onto the chain and are pulled upward. On rides such as Superman: Escape from Krypton at Six Flags Magic Mountain, California, linear motors do the job. These push and pull the cars along using magnetic fields just like maglev trains and their guideways. Superman can blast off from 0 to 100 miles (0 to 160 km) per hour in just seven seconds. Then, when the ride is at 415 feet (127 m) in the air, the only way is down!

This graphic from engineering company Thyssenkrupp gives an idea of the vertical and horizontal routes that maglev elevators could take through a building in the near future.

CUTTING EDGE

Hitachi has designed a magnetic elevator that will be superfast. When it is built, it will be able to travel up 95 floors in 43 seconds. That is 1,443 feet (440 m) and a speed of 45 miles (70 km) per hour. These elevators will have guide rollers, smooth braking, and other systems to make the ride feel smooth and keep passengers from feeling nauseous!

Some inventors think that using maglev technology to travel up a building or a roller coaster is small scale. They are thinking bigger and imagining using magnetic forces to even speed people up to space or between the continents!

THE MAGLIFTER

It is very expensive to send anything into space, because you need a space rocket and a lot of fuel. Currently, it costs about $10,000 to lift 2.2 pounds (1 kg) into space. Using a maglev launcher could lower this cost. The Maglifter is a spaceship, a little like the space shuttle, which is carried on a maglev sled. The sled speeds the spaceship up to 550 miles (885 km) per hour through a tube up a mountainside. Then, its engines push it onward to space. The spaceship does not need fuel or engine power. Once the spaceship has delivered its cargo to space, it can glide back to Earth. The Maglifter sled simply returns to the start of the tube to take off again.

CUTTING EDGE

If Maglifter would make space travel less expensive, Startram could make it a steal! Startram plans use magnetic levitation to hold up a vacuum tube that stretches from Earth into the atmosphere, through which a spaceship would travel. The tube would be 1,000 miles (1,600 km) long and reach an altitude of 12 miles (20 km). Using this, it would cost just $50 to send 2.2 pounds (1 kg) of cargo into space.

TRANSATLANTIC TUNNEL

Ideas for a massive tunnel to connect the United States and Europe have been around since the 1930s. But maglev technology may make high-speed transatlantic train travel possible. The idea is to suspend tunnels 150 to 300 feet (100 to 200 m) beneath the ocean surface, where the water pressure is not as dangerous as at deeper depths. The tunnels would be vacuums to reduce drag, and railcars would float inside using maglev technology. Magnetic forces in linear motors would pull cars along at up to 800 miles (1,287 km) per hour between the United Kingdom and New York City in just four hours.

This is an artist's impression of Startram, a spacecraft able to launch passengers and cargo into space using technology similar to that of the Maglifter.

THE POTENTIAL OF MAGLEV

Maglev is technology that is ready to be used more widely. It has great potential to become a major form of transportation in the near future on Earth and may even help us to reach other planets. Maglev is also part of the mix of solutions to transportation problems that we have today.

ADAPTABILITY

Maglev trains cause little pollution, use less energy, and can travel faster than other forms of ground transportation. They have many advantages over airplanes in time-saving and safety, too. Different maglev systems are adaptable for different situations, from slow automated EMS commuter trains to high-speed EDS express services. Superconductors allow inventors to make magnets strong enough to lift loaded trains. Future researchers might discover new materials that can provide powerful magnetic forces using even less power and find new ways to make maglevs travel even faster.

LOW-IMPACT TRANSPORT

Earth's climate is changing. There are more extreme weather events and the average global temperature is rising. This global warming is caused by the buildup of gases in the atmosphere produced by power stations and fuel-powered vehicles. Climate change impacts our planet in many ways. It melts ice sheets on which polar bears live and makes it more difficult for farmers to grow food. Maglev trains burn less fuel than regular trains. If we use renewable energy sources, such as wind and solar power, to make more of the power needed for the maglevs' electromagnets, we will also help slow climate change.

A glacier crumbling is one sign of global warming. In 2015, many countries committed to new targets for limiting climate change. Better transportation solutions such as maglev will be part of the solution.

CUTTING EDGE

In 2012, Chinese architect Wei Zhao designed an island that could float high above Earth using incredibly powerful electromagnets that repel Earth's magnetic field! The island, called Heaven and Earth, would spin as it floats and this movement would provide power to operate the electromagnets. His project was one idea presented to solve the overcrowding found in many cities on our planet.

GLOSSARY

aerodynamic having a shape that reduces drag

drag force of air resistance that pushes against objects moving forward

electrodynamic suspension (EDS) using magnetic fields on both the train and guideway to repel each other

electromagnetic induction the electricity produced in a coil of wire when it moves past a magnet

electromagnetic suspension (EMS) using magnetic attraction to lift a train

electromagnets materials that become magnetic when electrical current flows through or near them

friction a force produced when one surface moves over another

generators machines for converting mechanical energy into electrical energy

Halbach array arrangement of magnets that produces a stronger magnetic field on one side than the other

Inductrack technology that uses permanent magnets to cause lift in maglevs

Linimo a type of EMS maglev system used for slow commuter trains in Japan

magnetic field the region around a magnet where magnetic forces act

M-Bahn a maglev train line in Berlin in the early 1990s

repel when magnetic forces push objects apart

shinkansen Japanese high-speed train, usually requiring special track or guideway

superconductors materials that conduct electricity better than regular metals as long as they are kept very cold